WHO ATE MY CHEESE?

JOHN W NICHOLS

+ + +

WHO ATE MY CHEESE?

JOHN W NICHOLS

A nauseating treatise on cheese
and its consumption.

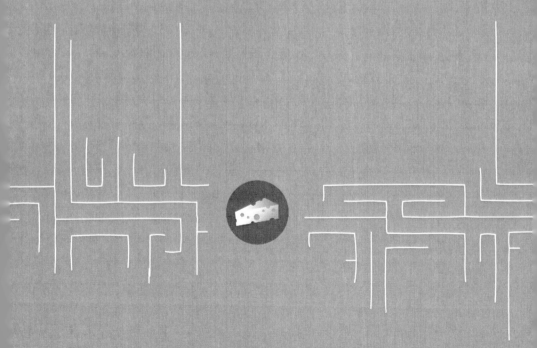

+ + +

ISBN: 978-1-4357-1220-1

FOREWORD +

Corporate executives love Spencer Johnson's masterpiece, *Who Moved My Cheese?* It seems to evoke warm fuzzy feelings that lend credence to their decisions to abuse and misuse the guys at the bottom of the corporate food chain, the lowly workers. The pond scum at the bottom of the corporate ladder should, in the eyes of management, be flexible, adjustable, adaptable and ready to do whatever the corporate heads demand. Complaints by workers, demands for accountability in management, or suggestions for improvement in the business picture are neither solicited nor welcomed. Employees should simply run around the maze looking for cheese, and jump into a new maze as often as required. Then all will be well with the world. For all you worker bees out there who are tired of assuming the corporate position, read on. This story is for you. This is "cheese" from another angle.

+ + +

To my wife Shawn, and my daughters Amanda and Michelle...
You are my treasures and my love is yours.

TABLE OF CONTENTS +

WHAT HAPPENED? +

Mike, Mark, Hunter, and Andy were four friends who met while employed by a large telecommunications company, Chaos.com. The foursome worked at the company for years and each expected his employment to continue until retirement. Comprehensive benefits coupled with good salaries, modest annual raises and even on occasion, bonuses, made working for Chaos.com a sweet deal. The friends drifted from assignment to assignment within the corporate portfolio of projects and focused their efforts on the simple goal of making the company profitable and successful. At times the four even entertained thoughts of having a son or daughter follow in their footsteps at Chaos.com. They hardly noticed the passing years.

Now they found themselves together again but not at Chaos.com. They were unemployed, a situation caused by something described in the trade press as "the bursting of the telecommunications bubble." Something happened at Chaos.com which forced upper management to undertake a resizing event, also known as a head count reduction, or a layoff. The friends found that life had taken a rather surprising turn as they were back in the job market after many years, not thinking about retirement but considering how to secure a job, any job, and cover the next payment on the mortgage. They still gathered once a week to trade interview stories and swap fast food coupons. But sooner or later the conversation moved around to the rise and fall of Chaos.com.

"So, what really happened," Andy asked. "How did a company at the top of its industry plummet into the penny stock ranks so quickly?"

"Right, that's what I want to know," Mike asked. "Do you guys have any more information on the big crash?"

Hunter, the wise guy of the group and the one who usually had the answers (or at least made something up), told his friends, "You have to read the book to understand where we are and how we got here. The book will explain what happened at Chaos.com and a dozen other telecommunications companies just like it"

"Book, what book?" Mike asked. "You mean someone figured out who stuck the pin in the telecommunications bubble and wrote a book about the sudden and massive deflation?"

"Must be the CEO since he is the only one not looking for work," Mark added. "I think he gets paid through the end of the decade no matter what happens to the company or any of its employees."

"Or maybe you are referring to one of those stock market books. You know the ones written by the analysts who lost a bundle and want to make it back by unloading their books on an unsuspecting public," Andy noted cynically.

"Guys, the book I am talking about is The Cheese Book", Hunter replied.

This comment really pushed Mark's button and he spewed, "I read that cheese book already. I know change happens. I also know some other things that happen and I didn't have to learn it from a book."

"No," Hunter shot back. "I mean the real cheese book, the book that tells the truth about cheese."

Andy said, "I have never heard of it but given the current economic situation I don't think I will be buying any books for a while. Maybe I can borrow it from the public library since that service is still free."

"Well, I think I can give you the main idea of the book if you have a little time to spare." Hunter started to talk and the others drew their chairs up closer so they could catch every word.

Hunter began, "We all know mice like cheese, right? There is a common misconception that cheese is found in a maze and that premise has been used to illustrate the changing nature of life."

"Cheese in a maze is usually placed there by someone who likes to torture mice. It is there to test and tantalize those mice, to drive them crazy as they run down one dead end after another until finally, through luck or skill, they find the cheese. And then the maze is changed so the process can start again."

Hunter continued, "The truth is cheese comes from a cheese mine where it must be dug from the ground one chunk at a time. This is the story of one of those mines, Cheese Incorporated, and the lowly workers who made it a success ..."

MEET SOME CHEESY CHARACTERS +

Cheese, Inc. was a medium sized company with a stellar record as a cheese producer. An inquisitive and astute person visiting the company would notice the employees of Cheese, Inc. fell into three categories:

GROUP 1: **SHAFTEES**

These are the company worker bees, the folks who actually do real work. Their efforts can be traced directly to revenue produced by marketable products and services.

GROUP 2: **SHAFTERS**

The second group is also known as surface dwellers at Cheese, Inc. The group includes managers of all kinds, process weenies, and chart makers. While it seems that no company can survive without an abundance of Shafters, it can be hard to track their efforts in any tangible way to revenue. In fact it is next to impossible to fathom exactly what some of the Shafters do in the company but no respectable cheese mine could exist without an abundance of these folks.

GROUP 3: **FORMERLINGS**

There are previous managers of Cheese, Inc. who are no longer on the payroll, who no longer provide any service or value to the cheese production, but who continue to get a share of the cheese. This bizarre arrangement is described by an obscure Latin word meaning "excellence" and the arrangement is excellent if you are the one getting free cheese. Formerlings consume a large share of the yearly cheese production and many of these formerlings meet together in what is known as a Bored of Misdirectors.

+ + +

At the lowest level of Cheese, Inc. is a Shaftee named Scoop and the company would collapse without his dedication to the job. Scoop is an expert at what he does—digging cheese. He loves his occupation and believes that Cheese, Inc. is a world class company. He wears shirts with the company logo and even has a company bumper sticker on his car. Scoop knows that a strong and successful company is the result of every employee giving 110%. He is a professional, and stands ready to share his knowledge with others who want to learn to dig cheese. Scoop is willing to put out extra effort to get around problems down in the mine and to apply his knowledge to deduce innovative solutions to challenges in cheese production. Scoop's philosophy is "I dig cheese", which may mean he likes cheese or it may just describe his attitude on the job.

A second and equally important Shaftee is Scoop's closest coworker, Scrapper, the corporate cheese hauler. Someone has to get the cheese out of the mine so that it can be stockpiled at the surface. It is a dirty job without a lot of glitter and glamour but Scrapper works endless hours filling a train of cheese carts, pushing, pulling, and tugging them out of the mine. Like Scoop, Scrapper loves his job and believes that there is no better place to work than Cheese, Inc.

The chief Shafter at Cheese, Inc. is known secretly by his employees as the Black Hole or BH for short. BH is a legend in his own mind. Though he has never worked in one, he did visit a mine one time when he got lost looking for a conference room. BH assumes himself to be an expert at every aspect of cheese mining although the truth is BH would not know how to dig cheese if his life depended on it. No one seems to know where he came from or how he got to the top of the corporate ladder but there are a lot of rumors.

BH likes to eat cheese, as much cheese as he can get and he never gets enough. BH calls this quest for cheese "integrity" which is from the Latin word meaning "whole" as in "I want the whole pile of cheese." BH loves to embrace cheesy sayings such as "Dig smarter, not harder" and he retains any cheese related buzz words he hears or reads. BH can deliver hours of meaningless speech by effortlessly stringing these buzz words together in never ending combinations.

BH loves to talk about the bottom line and the top line. Honestly, the more cheese one eats, the bigger his or her bottom line will be. No one seems to know what a top line is but current thought is this is the maximum number of shares of cheese awarded to BH in a given year.

Now that the characters are introduced, on with the story...

+ + +

IF YOU CAN'T

SMELL THE

CHEESE

SOMETHING

IS **WRONG.**

CHAPTER **1**

One day Scoop and Scrapper concluded they had been down in the mine long enough and it was time to collect their hard earned share of the cheese. They laid aside their tools and started up to the surface to begin a new chapter in life.

Scoop said, "I figure by now there must be a couple of huge piles of cheese with our names on them just waiting for us to savor."

Scrapper replied, "Well I know I have pulled enough cheese carts out of this mine over the years. It is time to leave this opportunity to the youngsters and enjoy the fruit of our labors."

The two cheesy workers exited the mine, allowed time for their eyes to adjust to the bright light, and then looked around expectantly to see that magnificent cheese.

"This is it," Scoop exhaled with delight. But as they looked around they saw nothing. There was no cheese, no crumbs of cheese, not even a cheesy scent in the air. The cheese was gone!

"What happened," wailed Scrapper, "Who ate my cheese?"

"This can't be right," Scoop replied in a low, quiet voice. He saw his dreams of retirement quickly going up in smoke.

The two coworkers sat down bewildered and angry and began to consider their long careers at Cheese, Inc. "How could this have happened?", Scoop demanded to know.

"I don't know but we are going to find out," Scrapper stated forcefully. "We will investigate, we will track down the sleazy cheese culprit or culprits, and we will publish our findings for the world to see! We must warn future cheese workers."

Scoop took a pen from his pocket, picked up his ever present note pad, and wrote his first observation:

If you can't smell the cheese, something is wrong.

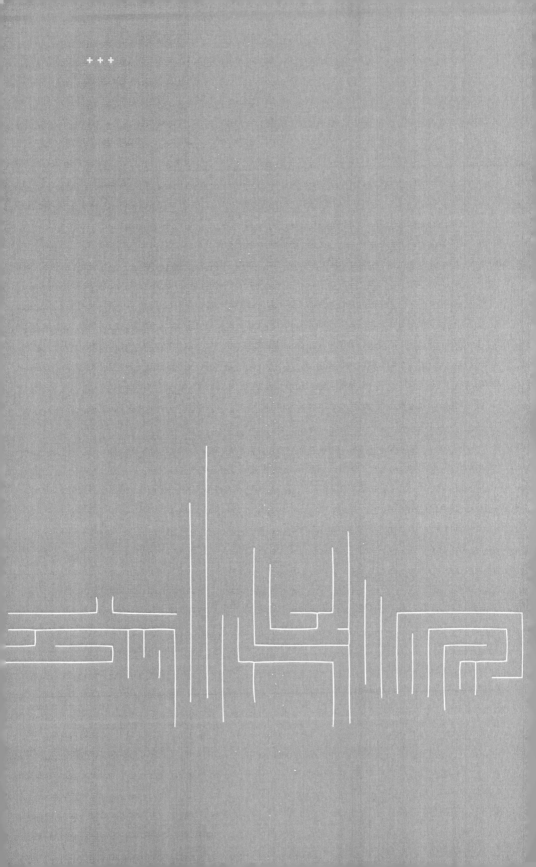

+ + +

IF YOU AREN'T

GETTING

CHEESE

GET OUT

OF THE MINE.

CHAPTER **2**

As Scoop and Scrapper wandered among the ruins of Cheese, Inc. looking for cheesy clues, they found a poster BH once hung on the wall. It read "Work is its own reward." They both recalled this was one of BH's favorite sayings. He came up with the line the first time he wanted Scoop and Scrapper to work more hours in the mine for no additional share of the cheese. BH decided that a bigger cheese pile would not be important to Scoop and Scrapper and hundreds like them, that moving cheese was their life and that they would even work for free since they loved mining cheese so much.

BH was a master at manipulating workers and he invented "24X7", a now famous productivity initiative. He was confident this plan would allow Scoop and Scrapper to achieve personal satisfaction while they worked harder for less cheese in the larder. Since BH knew his people were the strength of any great cheese organization, "24x7" would empower Scoop and Scrapper to work 7 free hours for every 24 they logged in the mine. It would allow them to focus energy on something called ownership in the corporation as they produced over and beyond their usual efforts.

BH was always thinking about his employees and what was best for them and he knew if they had free time outside work they might get into some entangling trouble like getting married and raising a family, coaching a kid's ball team or volunteering as a mentor in the local school system. It would be far better to have exhausted, weary workers who came to work tired, stayed far too long then staggered straight home to bed. Those workers are easier to manipulate. BH coerced Scoop and Scrapper to work more and more hours by telling them they were professionals and their salary covered the whole job, not just a certain number of hours. BH decided the bounds of the whole job and his interpretation would then become the goal of the harried workers.

Scoop and Scrapper shook their heads as they remembered all the late nights and weekends they thought they had invested in a brighter future. Yes, they had embraced "24x7" and yes, they had swallowed the line that it would lead to higher profits and a larger cheese pile. Now they understood the larger cheese pile was for someone else.

Scoop jotted down another revelation:

If you aren't getting a fair share of the cheese, get out of the mine.

+ + +

YOU CAN'T **DIG**

CHEESE

IF YOU'RE STUCK

IN **MEETINGS**

ALL DAY.

CHAPTER **3**

Scattered throughout the rubble of what was once the mighty empire of Cheese, Inc., Scoop and Scrapper found pieces of conference tables and the remains of conference chairs. The guys remembered the hours wasted in the most prolific activity at Cheese, Inc., meetings. Company employees who did not actually dig or handle cheese (surface dwellers) had to spend their days doing something so they could feel a sense of accomplishment, value and worth. The solution to this issue was the creation of the meeting!

Surface dwellers considered it a great day at the office if their schedule was completely filled with meetings, pre-meetings, and meetings to decide the agenda of the pre-meetings. It was not known if anything useful, anything which aided in cheese production or increased profits ever resulted from the meetings but meetings were self perpetuating. A good meeting generated "keep busy" work for many of the attendees. There were agendas to publish before the meeting (but no one ever read them!). There were "action items", extra work awarded to some attendees to be completed after the meeting. There were follow up meetings to review progress on the action items. Sometimes meetings had to be cancelled due to the absence of "key players" who were mysterious and lofty people divinely gifted with a level of knowledge beyond that of mere mortals. The presence of a key player a meeting was necessary to certify any outcome as valid.

BH loved to pull Scoop and Scrapper away from their work in the mine to attend some of these meetings, especially staff meetings. A staff meeting is a senseless gathering where attendees gather in a tiny room and snuggle up close to one another to swap staff germs (or any other kind of germ they may have). This meeting was designed to aid in sharing whatever bug was active among any of the attendees. Staff meetings were usually held in a room having (x-3) chairs where x is the number of bodies invited to the meeting. Staff meetings never started and stopped on a time schedule and never followed a published agenda. Avoiding staff meetings to continue productive work would earn a Shaftee the description, "He is not a team player."

Staff meetings gave BH the chance to find out what Scoop and Scrapper did during the previous week. It might seem that BH actually cared and wanted to assist in the cheese production but he really needed to know what work had been done so that he could report it and take credit for it at the next Manager's Only meeting. Cheese Inc. held a lot of Manager's Only meetings and no one ever figured out what went on behind those closed doors.

Scoop took out his pen and captured another profound thought:

You can't dig cheese if you're stuck in meetings all day.

+++

THE MORE YOU

WANT THE

CHEESE

THE LOWER YOU

MAY STOOP

TO **GRAB** IT.

CHAPTER 4

BH always told his workers, "More cheese does not buy more happiness." As he surveyed the ruins of Cheese, Inc, Scrapper now understood that BH meant other people having cheese did not make BH happy.
A person chasing cheese which does not belong to him would usually cause a diversion so no one could realize the cheese was disappearing. BH had several smoke screens that he used to cover his cheese hording activities.

It would seem obvious to any observer (MBA or not) that increased profits could be found in decreasing production costs or increasing production efficiencies. Cheese diggers with the latest equipment and training could produce more cheese, and hence the company would have more cheese to sell. BH had no interest in increasing efficiency. In fact he was insistent that workers buy their own tools and equipment. He further mandated that there would be no company funded office supplies. Paper, pens, gloves, shovels, or any other day-to-day requirements for the job would come from the Shaftees' personal funds. It was, after all, a privilege to work for Cheese, Inc. The company did provide toilet paper, allowed workers access to free flushing toilets, and once in a while included soap in the restrooms. The entire cheese budget for tools and supplies was swept into BH's personal stash and used to provide premium tools and equipment in the corporate offices. In his mind he was saving the company money by not outfitting the workers and he therefore deserved the nicest perks.

At Cheese Inc. no one knew how to start a panic like BH. He would issue a memo detailing a cheese production schedule required to fill some order already promised to a customer. Factors like "Is it physically possible to dig and prepare cheese to meet those dates with the current staff levels?" were never consider in these schedules. At no time did BH considered physical limits like work output per person, availability of mine cars, or trip time per load coming up from the mine. This management genius never considered new tools and techniques which might increase worker productivity. He just yelled, ranted, and raved ... and made more schedules.

Scoop and Scrapper both knew the old adage that "hind sight is always 20/20" so BH must have started with the end date and worked backwards to derive his schedules. BH was a smart one and given the usual location of his head, hind sight came naturally.

"Surely he never used random dates in the scheduling process," Scrapper said. "I can still hear him ranting that the world will end or raving that heads will roll, or prophesying that the market window would close if we didn't deliver on time."

Scoop reminded him, "Yea, but we made every date and we did whatever was required to meet those schedules. And the cheese has still disappeared."

During times when cheese was not moving, (and if one eats too much of it that could be anytime), BH struggled to find ways to keep his cheese share increasing. At times he would fire 3 or 4 shaft workers and declare himself an efficiency bonus. Scoop and Scrapper realized that there were no limits to the tactics BH used to gain more cheese.

With a heavy heart Scoop recorded another clue to the cheese mystery:

The more you want the cheese, the lower you may stoop to grab it.

YOU CAN'T **GET**

CHEESE

WITHOUT A LITTLE

DIGGING.

CHAPTER **5**

Scoop and Scrapper knew Cheese would not dig itself. If there was going to be a pile of cheese to sell and share, someone had to go into the mine and get it. Without those loyal searchers, production would grind to a halt, and profits would drop. Scoop recalled that even though the cheese workers were so vital to the profits they were always the first to be forced into the state of being surplus. The concept of being surplus had mysterious factors associated with it like head count, target sizes, budget and so forth. It can best be summed up with this simple thought—if you are the guy who works in the shaft you will get it in the end.

BH and his band of merry cohorts invested hours trying to find ways to make more cheese happen without the inconvenience and expense of paying workers to mine it. They decided to cut costs and any competent MBA knows the solution to cutting costs is to have weekly reorganizations. These were seemingly random staff shuffles in the operations of Cheese, Inc. and each was touted as the harbinger of upcoming profits. How staff reorganizations could provide more cheese to sell and increase profits was a question no shaft worker could answer. Logic and common sense dictated that more profits would come as more cheese was sold or production costs were lowered. BH loved to play "name that group" as teams and projects were named, renamed, and then given new names again to confuse the most tenacious investigator. Managers moved from group to group like politicians seeking voters, organizational charts were printed in all the colors of the rainbow, and unexpected shortfalls in quarterly sales figures always meant it was time for another shuffle.

When random reorganizations did not yield the desired profits, BH decided to invest some of the company's cheese is a new corporate logo. He figured if the community of customers recognized Cheese Inc., it would encourage them to buy more cheese from Cheese, Inc. BH hired an expensive advertising agency to design the new logo and waited anxiously for the final result. Unknown to BH, the agency forgot completely about Cheese, Inc.'s new logo and had to slam something together in a last minute design effort. The final logo looked suspiciously like the imprint an overflowing coffee cup may make on a napkin but BH loved it. After all he had used the company's cheese to finance its creation and to express displeasure with the "Coffee Ring" would border on admitting a mistake. That was a path no self exalted surface dweller would ever undertake.

Scoop shivered as he thought of the one word which struck fear into the hearts of any Shaftee, the "P" word—process. At Cheese Inc., process was given the name ISwear9001 and process was king in cheese production. ISwear9001 covered documented techniques for digging cheese, explained the one and only one right way to hold and use a shovel, and covered the safe way to move cheese by bending at the knees and not the waist. Every stage of the process was thoroughly documented and ISwear9001 required the completion of various forms and reviews before the cheese could move to the next higher level. Cheese production efficiencies were slashed to ¼ of the pre-process figures but the Shafters maintained that following the process would eventually yield greater profits.

The process at Cheese, Inc. even specified a series of steps required to adjust anything within the process itself. The changer must fill out a Change Request Approval Paper, and then appear before a Change Request Approval Panel to justify the desired change. In short, one had to go through CRAP to make a change.

Scoop followed his process and recorded another observation:

You can't get cheese without a little digging.

+ + +

NOT **EVERYONE**

LIKES THE

SAME KIND OF

CHEESE.

CHAPTER **6**

There were hundreds of kinds of cheese in production at the apex of Cheese, Inc.'s dynasty and consumers who bought the cheese had their own preferences and needs. It was a tough job knowing which cheese would sell at any given time, which mine needed to be worked on any given day, how much cheese to dig, and when the customer required their cheese.

Scoop and Scrapper always thought there were employees meeting with cheese customers and asking questions to determine what Cheese, Inc. should produce. After all, if cheddar was in demand one week it would not pay to dig American. The challenge was to figure out what the customer needed and wanted and then arrange production accordingly. Everyone made out in the end and happy customers always returned to Cheese, Inc. for more quality cheese. There seemed to be no bounds to the ever expanding revenue stream.

Down in the shaft, Scoop and Scrapper never had much chance to talk to real customers and ask the important questions. Scoop recalled, "I don't think I ever saw a customer down in the cheese mine."

"I saw a few tour groups but we were not allowed to talk with them. In fact customers were only allowed to tour in specially controlled demonstration shafts. They were never in the real mine," Scrapper noted. "That would violate insurance regulations or may allow trade secrets to be compromised."

For a time, Cheese, Inc. had top notch folks doing the very important job of meeting with customers to determine their needs. Talking to customers was a priority and gaining understanding into the ways cheese was used in their market was vital to Cheese, Inc.'s survival. There was real respect and admiration for an employee who could figure out the customer's application and recommend the best cheese for the task. But that all started to change one dreadful day. The Shaftees had worked diligently to fulfill a rush order for a certain kind of cheese only to discover that there was no customer waiting. No one had actually gotten an order for the cheese and so it sat in a pile at the surface and spoiled. But strangely enough, the Shafter who arranged the project, who allocated the resources and specified the order as the company's number one priority was given a bonus for the rapid production and speedily promoted.

All the two weary workers remembered after that was continually changing priorities—"dig this cheese, no wait we want that kind, ummm, really you better stop and give us the other kind."

These false productions would not have been a problem if a single mine held every variety of cheese. But a different shaft had to be dug and set up to mine each kind of cheese. This was a costly and time consuming challenge. Different skills were required to dig each cheese variety as well, and handling methods had to be adjusted as cheese type changed. False starts ate into the company's profits and resources began to be allocated based on a particular Shafter's argument that he knew which kind of cheese the market needed. Customers were forgotten and the art of listening to customers was dismissed as no longer necessary.

Cheese, Inc. started to produce the cheese with the highest profit margin even if that was not what the customers wanted. Then there were creative selling tactics such as financing the cheese purchase for a customer if needed and of course the customer's ability to honor the financial commitment was never part of the consideration. Moving cheese in shady deals meant big bonus for Shafters but it also meant rapid erosion of the company's financial health.

Shafters learned quickly that short term personal gains could be made at the expense of the company's long term future. The company sagged, the product quality degraded, the workers grew despondent and all the while the bonus checks piled up for the Shafters. At least someone was happy.

The realization dawned on the two Shaftees that maybe the Shafters were not so smart after all. Now all of them were out of work, missing their cheese.

Scrapper kicked at a pile of crumbled papers and a memo from BH caught his eye. It was a recommendation to the Bored of Misdirectors on additional staff cuts to maximize profits. And those cuts were to come from the ranks of the workers who knew and met with customers. These were "surplus positions, non-essential tasks."

The memo continued, "We will produce quantities of every kind of cheese our mines offer and have it ready for sale at any given time. If we don't have a particular kind of cheese we can quickly buy a neighboring mine for a premium price and complete our cheese portfolio. That way no matter what cheese a customer wants, we can have it."

"And now we know why there were always piles of rotting cheese wasting at the surface." Scoop intoned.

"Yep," Scrapper responded, "We tried to make people eat cheese they didn't want."

"And we dug like crazy thinking that the market must be really hot," Scoop shared. "What a scam. What a waste."

He took out his pen and wrote:

Not every one likes the same kind of cheese.

+ + +

YOU MAY **KEEP**

MORE OF YOUR

CHEESE

IF YOU STOP

TO SNIFF IT ONCE

IN A WHILE.

CHAPTER **7**

Scoop saw that Shaftees at Cheese, Inc. tended to focus too deeply on the job at hand. They spent too many hours in the mine and forgot that the reason for working is to earn cheese and enjoy life. Cheese makes the world go around and although some say it will not buy happiness, a little cheese can sure make life run more smoothly.

Cheese, Inc. compensated its workers in various ways including salary, bonuses, awards, and a company sponsored savings plan. Shaftees had been reminded regularly that the company compensation package was in the bottom 10% of the top 50% of companies paying less money than its competitors. Employees of Cheese, Inc. were fortunate to be part of such a world class organization.

Scoop readily admitted that salary was a big reason he worked so hard at Cheese, Inc. He believed that raises would come in proportion to his work output. Now he and Scrapper sat on a pile of old binders and read a top secret company document they found under a trash can—the company's "Guide to Compensation."

According to the secret tome, raises were determined annually by some very scientific means. First, an analysis of recruiting trends let the Shafters know which workers were likely to make more money at a competitor and hence leave Cheese, Inc. Then all workers were evaluated on their previous year's contributions against some random standards derived 2 days before the evaluation. Next, there was the ranking of all employees into a top to bottom list. Lastly the Shafters would gather in a large conference room and show pictures of each employee. If the employee's picture created a desire on any Shafter's part to laugh, then that Shaftee was disqualified from further raise considerations until the next year. Each Shafter had to explain why his person deserved a better raise than everyone else. If a Shafter did not show up for the fight, or showed up but did not fight for his people, they got the shaft. After the ranking was completed, a procedure which could take several pre-meetings, meetings, and follow up meetings, the Shafters took 10% of the raise pot and divided it equally among the Shaftees who would be participating in salary planning that year. No one ever figured out where the other 90% went.

Cheese Inc. boasted a bountiful bonus bonanza. Employees could earn extra money by working harder and delivering more cheese. Shafters would share the company profits with Shaftees but of course the Shaftee share was very tiny, in fact, just a crumb. Scoop found the page which showed the formula used by Shafters to determine the amount of a Shaftee's bonus:

Number day of the week * losing team's score in Super Bowl III * Universal Obfuscation Factor * Freezing point of water in degrees C * 1.234534% of company income for the previous quarter.

Cheese, Inc. sported many cash award programs to recognize exemplary employees. Scrapper looked at the list and read Manager of the Year, Managerial Innovation Award, Rankest Ranker Award, Shafter Par Excellence and so on. "Hmmm," Scrapper murmured, "These are all for Shafters."

Cheese, Inc. was a progressive, modern concern which offered its workers a company sponsored cheese savings program called 401Pray. The first 400 plans did not work very well, hence plan number 401. Each worker could set aside a portion of his or her cheese to be invested in cheese funds chosen by the company. The company would add a matching share of cheese to the worker's contribution and the worker's net pile was expected to grow by leaps and bounds. It seemed like a good idea to most Shaftees especially since some wise financial Misdirector would see to it that the cheese contributions were invested for rapid and maximum expansion.

Scoop captured his latest note:

You may keep more of your cheese if you take time to sniff it once in a while.

+ + +

CHEESE

BY ANY

OTHER NAME

STILL

SMELLS.

CHAPTER **8**

Shafters at Cheese, Inc. were always concerned about the company's image in the community. They figured that a well known company would command higher profits and attract top talent in the cheese industry.

Scrapper surveyed the empty office waste land that was once home to hundreds of cheese workers and felt the lonely breeze on his face. He said, "Well I guess everyone knows Cheese, Inc. now."

"Right," Scoop added, "No other company has lost so much cheese in so short a time."

"Only the government could go through cheese faster," Scrapper replied.

The two began to reminisce about the fluff used by Shafters at Cheese, Inc. to transform the company name into a household word.

Millions had been spent on television commercials which made no sense and had no point. No one could tell what products Cheese, Inc. marketed by watching these ads but the company logo was flashed in nearly every scene coupled with cool music to capture attention. Someone thought it was a good idea, probably the advertising agency.

The company logo was also plastered on bus station restroom stalls right above the armored toilet paper dispensers. "And what moron came up with the catch phrase: 'We wipe the competition at Cheese Inc?' " Scoop pondered.

One competitor of Cheese, Inc. suggested that all cheese production facilities should give something back to the community and so wiggling up from the swamp of bad ideas came the United Play.

United Play was another way that Formerlings could increase their share of cheese without actually working. Every employee of a cheese factory was asked to donate 5% of his cheese share to United Play. This donation was to be voluntary and no reprisals would befall an employee who decided not to participate, except that nonparticipation would result in an entry being made onto an employee's permanent record card that he or she was not a team player, a stigma that would never be erased.

Various Formerlings from these cheese mines who some how found their way to becoming well paid employees of United Play, gathered all the cheese and took responsibility for its disbursements.

Of course, United Play had to have executive office space, and United Play officials had to jet about in rented luxury aircraft and visit exotic locations for think sessions where they could derive such witticisms as "we use your cheese like it was our own."

Once in a while a United Play executive would make the news having been caught hiding 90% of the cheese contributions in his own cheese vaults while putting the other 10% into charities around the community. Usually the official was banned from further cheese collecting activities for United Play and was forced to run for public office.

United Play made Shafters at Cheese, Inc. feel good about themselves and their company. Cheese, Inc. had been the largest contributor to the fund for 6 years running and each year the Shafters spent more and more cheese promoting the annual collection. They would raffle off cars and trips, would give away their executive parking places and once in a while would even make the ultimate sacrifice and let a lowly Shaftee who contributed to the United Play fund make use of the executive washroom. It was rumored that the company stocked high quality paper towels in the executive facility instead of the recycled newspaper with wood splinters that was provided for employees.

Scoop commented, "You know if the company had added up all the cheese they spent promoting the annual cheese collection and just wrote a check for that amount to the fund it would probably have doubled the total contributions.

Scrapper commented, "We should never have allowed the company to get distracted from the prime directive of digging cheese."

Scoop penned a summary statement:

Cheese by any other name still smells.

+ + +

PLAYING WITH

CHEESE

TOYS IS MORE

FUN THAN

WORKING.

CHAPTER **9**

Scrapper moved a pile of old cheese wrappers and out tumbled a collection of beautiful multi-color charts.

"Wow, Scrapper, what have you found now?" Scoop asked.

"Charts—the Shafter's delight," Scrapper replied, "And in color no less."

The two friends remembered Shafters always seemed to have the latest technology sitting on their desks—powerful computers with the high resolution monitors, color printers that doubled as shredders, and drawers filled with state of the art cheese cutting devices. And sadly none of these high tech cheese tools ever touched a slab of cheese.

Cheese production techniques had improved through the years and new tools and equipment had potential for increasing profits. But buying tools meant spending cheese and Shafters would never agree to that. Tools had always been viewed as too expensive especially just to send into the mine to get dirty. Shafters felt a need to remain current with industry developments so they could talk about the newest trends over lunch. They could attend trade conferences, read trade journals, and try out new tools. Those same tools which were too expensive for the mine shafts were affordable necessities on the desks of the Shafters. For them playing technology was a game to win and there were no limits.

"I wonder how much cheese was wasted on tools and equipment never used in real production", Scoop pondered.

"We will never know", was Scrapper's reply.

Scoop added another note to his list:

Playing with Cheese toys is more fun than working.

✦ ✦ ✦

WHAT NEXT? +

"Oh, I feel sick," Mark moaned.

"It's probably those bran muffins," Mike replied. "I warned you not to eat so many."

"It's not the muffins. It's the realization that the signs were there all along. If we had just opened our eyes we could have seen that the Shafters at Chaos.com were eating all the cheese," Mark commented. "We might have pulled some money out and put it into another fund or something."

"The most obvious problem to me was the CEO taking home 50% of the company's yearly income as a bonus. And the size of his bonus was tied to fluctuations in the stock price rather than actual income levels", Andy observed.

"There you go. So he did whatever it took to move the stock price in the short term rather than working towards a long term goal", Hunter said.

"Like canceling key designs and cutting customer interactions so that only "Shafters" could visit and talk with customers", Mark blurted, "No wonder we worked on so many projects which never sold. We were digging cheese nobody wanted."

Andy looked at the others and asked, "Assuming we can get back to work in this industry, how do we keep it from happening at the next company? What can we do to be proactive?"

Mike piped in "I plan to sniff my cheese on a regular basis. You know, read the trade press more closely, especially keep up with products being offered by competitors. If my company is not developing applications in similar areas, it might be a sign we are falling behind. I also need to watch the actual sales numbers and make sure that revenue is being derived from customer dollars, not creative accounting."

Mark tilted his head and looked down his nose at the others to state, "I will only work for a world class company that values its employees and rewards innovation."

Andy smirked, "Why don't you go leverage an installed base or shift a paradigm or something? You sound like a Shafter."

Mark retorted, "I'm serious. What good is working for a company on a long term basis if in the end you are downsized, loose your seniority, and so on? It would be better to focus on the technology, maintain my skill set at peak efficiency and move within the company as required so I work in current and marketable arenas. That way if the bubble pops again I might have skills in demand by other concerns. Mining cheese is not the only way to make a living you know."

"Hmmm! You may be on to something there. Why be loyal to my company if all it gets me is shafted?" Mike added.

Hunter shared, "I have considered trade unions like the miners and the auto workers have. Maybe telecommunications workers need something like that. There are plusses and minuses but at least we could force management to be more accountable."

"But engineers and software writers are not joiners," Mark chipped in. "It would be impossible to get a group to stand together and fight the company. Besides, if we tried to organize or strike, our jobs would just be outsourced to someone who would work for a lower wage."

Andy came back, "Well that is happening anyway. Maybe it is time to start flooding our elected representatives with calls, letters, visits, and emails. We can demand protection for jobs here at home."

Mike winced and replied, "And many of those elected representatives get major cheese piles from the very Shafters and Misdirectors that brought the industry down. Their loyalties are to the money, not the voter."

"Right, and how can lowly workers hold the Shafters who make up the Board of Misdirection accountable? What will we do, threaten to withhold their bonus checks? I don't see that happening," Andy commented.

Hunter thought for a minute and suggested, "One idea is to look at tools and equipment used by workers in a company—are they state of the art? Bargain basement operations that scrimp on tools will also look at technology workers as a commodity to be hired and fired on a whim. Corporate managers forget all the time that the intellectual value of an experienced worker does not show up on a balance sheet. We are simply a commodity to be bought and used as needed.

Mark thought for a few minutes and said, "I am not sure there are any easy answers. We aren't guaranteed a job anymore or that the job will last a certain number of years. And people in other countries want to share in the bounty of a good standard of living. Maybe things will level out after a few years as salaries in those places rise.

+ + +

Manufactured by Amazon.ca
Acheson, AB

13017071R00035